D0686744

Black, Carolyn.
Pakistan : the people /
c2003.
33305203286343
CU   05/13/03

PAKISTAN
the people

Carolyn Black

A Bobbie Kalman Book

The Lands, Peoples, and Cultures Series

Cra[b]...ompany

SANTA CLARA COUNTY LIBRARY

3 3305 20328 6343

The Lands, Peoples, and Cultures Series

Created by Bobbie Kalman

Coordinating editor
Ellen Rodger

Production coordinator
Rosie Gowsell

Project development, photo research, design, and editing
First Folio Resource Group, Inc.
   Erinn Banting
   Tom Dart
   Söğüt Y. Güleç
   Greg Duhaney
   Jaimie Nathan
   Debbie Smith

Prepress and printing
Worzalla Publishing Company

Consultants
Dr. Naeem Ahmed, Vice Consul, Consulate General of
Pakistan, Toronto; David Butz, Department of Geography,
Brock University; Nancy Cook; Tahira Naqvi, Westchester
Community College and New York University; Dr. Naren
Wagle, Center for South Asian Studies, University of Toronto

Photographs
Piers Benatar/Panos Pictures: p. 12 (right), p. 19 (bottom); Nigel
Blythe/Robert Harding: p. 20 (left); David Butz: p. 30, p. 31
(both); Gordon Clements/Axiom Photographic Agency: p. 28
(left); Neil Cooper/Panos Pictures: title page; Corbis/Magma
Photo News, Inc./Bettman: p. 9; Corbis/Magma Photo News,
Inc./Jonathan Blair: p. 26; Corbis/Magma Photo News, Inc.
/Hulton-Deutsch Collection, Inc.: p. 10; Corbis/Magma Photo
News, Inc./Christine Osborne: p. 3; Corbis/Magma Photos
News, Inc/Reuters New Media Inc.: p. 24 (right); Corbis/
Magma Photo News, Inc./Galen Rowell: p. 14; Tony Deane/
Bruce Coleman Inc.: p. 20 (right); Ric Ergenbright: p. 4 (right),
p. 18; Sarah Errington/Hutchison Library: p. 19 (top); Alain
Evrard/Robert Harding: p. 5 (bottom); Robert Harding: cover,
p. 6, p. 22 (bottom), p. 23 (left); Juliet Highet/Hutchison Library:
p. 27; Fred Hoogervorst/Panos Picutres: p. 21 (right); Ed Kashi:
p. 11, p. 24 (left), p. 25 (bottom), p. 28 (right); Titus Moser/
Hutchison Library: p. 12 (left); Sarah Murray/Hutchison Library:
p. 15, p. 22 (top); North Wind Pictures: p. 8; Christine Osborne:
p. 13 (both), p. 16 (both), p. 17 (right), p. 29 (both); D. Sansoni/
Panos Pictures: p. 4 (left); Ron Schroeder: p. 5 (top); Trip/D.
Burrows: p. 21 (left); Trip/Trip: p. 7, p. 17 (left), p. 23 (right);
Brian A. Vikander: p. 25 (top)

Illustrations
Dianne Eastman: icon
David Wysotski, Allure Illustrations: back cover

Cover: Camels are useful for travel in Pakistan's deserts.
They can carry people or heavy loads for hours without
food or rest.

Title page: Hindu sisters living near the Thar Desert, in the
southeast, wear loose clothing to keep cool.

Icon: Pots of spices appear at the head of each section.
Colorful, fragrant spices such as coriander, cumin, and chili
are used to flavor many traditional Pakistani dishes.

Back cover: The Indus River dolphin is one of the few
freshwater dolphins in the world, and it lives only in
Pakistan. This species of dolphin swims on its side, which
allows it to swim in shallow parts of the Indus River.

Published by
Crabtree Publishing Company

PMB 16A,
350 Fifth Avenue
Suite 3308
New York
N.Y. 10118

612 Welland Avenue
St. Catharines
Ontario, Canada
L2M 5V6

73 Lime Walk
Headington
Oxford OX3 7AD
United Kingdom

Copyright © **2003 CRABTREE PUBLISHING COMPANY.**
All rights reserved. No part of this publication may be
reproduced, stored in a retrieval system or transmitted in any
form or by any means, electronic, mechanical, photocopying,
recording, or otherwise, without the prior written permission
of Crabtree Publishing Company.

Library of Congress Cataloging-in-Publication Data
Black, Carolyn.
   Pakistan. The people / Carolyn Black.
      p. cm. -- (Lands, peoples, and cultures series)
   Includes index.
      Summary: Explores how the history, climate, geography,
   and religion of Pakistan have shaped the customs and
   practices of modern daily life.
      ISBN 0-7787-9347-8 (rlb. : alk. paper) -- ISBN 0-7787-9715-5
   (pb. : alk. paper)
      1. Pakistan--Social life and customs--Juvenile literature.
   [1. Pakistan--Social life and customs.] I. Title. II. Series.
   DS393.8 .B55 2003
   954.91--dc21
                                        2002013739
                                        LC

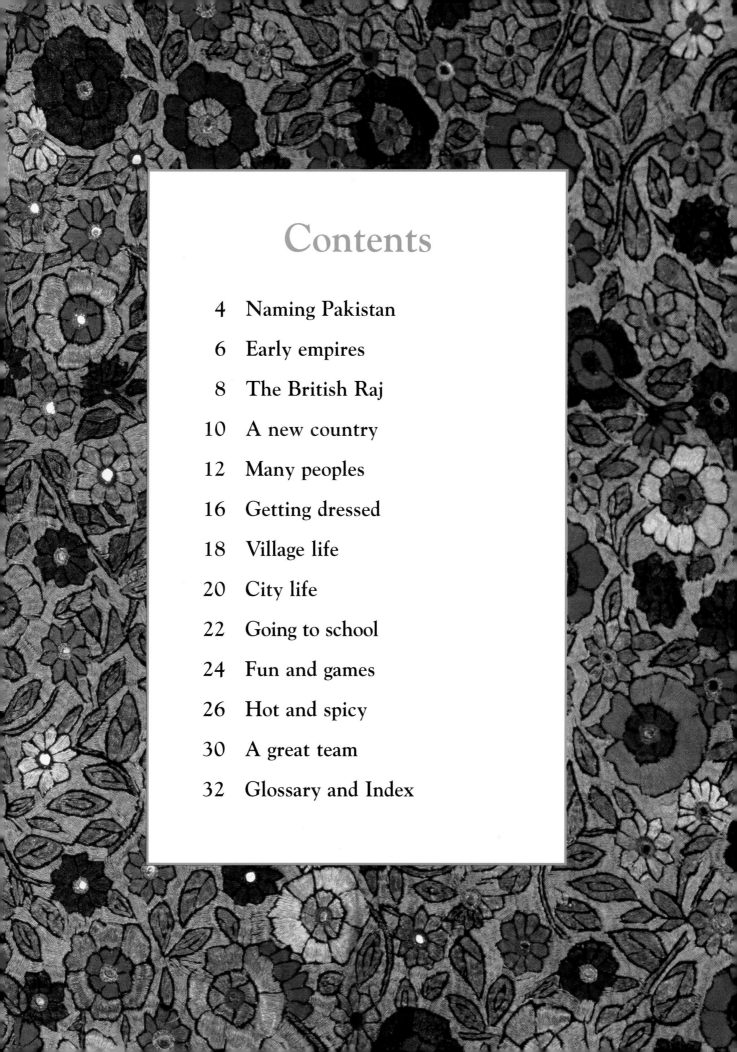

Contents

Naming Pakistan

Although most Pakistanis share the Muslim religion, they lead many different ways of life. Some herd animals on dry **plateaus** or cool mountains, some farm in small villages along the **fertile** banks of the Indus River, and some live in large cities where they work in office buildings or factories.

A family walks in fields outside Gilgit, the capital of the Northern Areas. The region is popular with tourists who climb the surrounding mountains and fish for trout in the many lakes and streams.

Men in Pakistan wear turbans in many different styles. You can sometimes tell where a man lives and what job he has by the way he wears his turban.

Pakistan means "land of the pure" in Urdu, the national language of Pakistan. The country was founded in 1947 as a **homeland** for **Muslims** who had lived in India under British rule for almost 200 years. According to one explanation, Pakistan's name was made up of letters from the names of regions that existed when it became a country: P for Punjab, or Panjab, in the central east; A for Afghania, in the northwest; K for Kashmir, in the northeast; S for Sind, in the southeast; and TAN for Baluchistan, in the west.

Friends from Rawalpindi, in the province of Punjab, enjoy time off during their summer vacation.

A citrus vendor in Lahore, a city in the east, sells refreshing drinks on a hot day.

The ancient village of Mehrgarh, in the center of Pakistan, was one of the first farming villages in the world. People lived there between 7000 B.C. and 2000 B.C. They grew wheat and barley, and raised cattle. Around the time that Mehrgarh disappeared, many large cities, such as Harappa and Mohenjo-daro, sprang up nearby. These cities, which lay along the banks of the Indus River, were home to the inhabitants of the enormous Indus Valley civilization. In about 1500 B.C., a **plague**, flood, or change in climate forced the people of the Indus Valley to leave their cities. They scattered throughout the countryside, and their civilization vanished.

Aryans

Aryans came to Pakistan from the west and northwest. They began arriving in 1500 B.C. and continued to come in waves for the next 1,000 years, spreading through Pakistan and moving east into India. Each Aryan group established its own kingdom, but all groups used the same language — an early form of Sanskrit. Their rituals and beliefs developed into the Hindu religion. Hindus believe in a creator power named Brahman, as well as many gods and goddesses whom they consider to be different forms of Brahman. They also believe that certain animals, especially cows, are holy.

Asoka's rule

In the third century B.C., an emperor named Asoka ruled the region of Gandhara, which included Pakistan and India. Asoka followed Buddhism, a religion that teaches people to rid themselves of evil by practicing good deeds and thinking good thoughts. He built huge stone pillars and carved teachings of the Buddha, the founder of Buddhism, into them. For hundreds of years after Asoka died, people in northern Pakistan continued to practice Buddhism. They built Buddhist **monasteries**, and carved statues of the Buddha and scenes from his life into the sides of mountains.

Ancient petroglyphs, or stone carvings, of Buddhist symbols decorate the cliffs outside the northern village of Chilas. Dust from the extremely hot valley coats the cliffs and turns them brown. The dust also preserves the carvings, which is why they are still so clear after thousands of years.

Invaders from the mountains

High, rugged mountains rise along Pakistan's north and west borders. For hundreds of years, invaders crossed these mountains into Pakistan through narrow passages called passes. Many invading armies, including armies led by the Persian king Darius in 518 B.C. and the Macedonian king Alexander the Great in 326 B.C., traveled through a rocky pass in the north called the Khyber Pass. Not all armies stayed in Pakistan. Some moved east to the more fertile **plains** of India. Armies that did remain established kingdoms, which were sometimes conquered by another army a few hundred years later. By 700 A.D., both Pakistan and India were divided into many kingdoms, each controlled by a different ruler.

The Mughal Empire

A new wave of Asian invaders entered Pakistan in the eighth century A.D. These invaders were Muslims. Muslims believe in one god, called Allah, and in his **prophet** Muhammad. Allah's commands are written in a holy book, the *Qur'an*. The Muslim invaders fought and defeated many Hindu rulers across the Indian **subcontinent**, and took over their kingdoms.

In 1525, Babur, who was a Muslim ruler from Central Asia, invaded Pakistan. With an army of 12,000 men, he defeated the other Muslim rulers in two years. Babur founded the Mughal dynasty, a family of powerful Muslim emperors who ruled for more than 200 years. They built forts, palaces, large gardens, and **mosques** throughout their cities. They also encouraged art, music, and literature.

Akbar the Great

Babur's grandson, Akbar, became emperor at the age of thirteen. In 1585, he moved the capital of his empire from Fatehur-Sikri, in northcentral India, to Lahore, in eastern Pakistan. There, he built a large, stone fort to protect the city from attack. During his reign, Akbar captured a great deal of territory, but treated those he conquered well as long as they recognized him as the emperor. He showed an interest in other religions, and invited scholars, poets, painters, and musicians to his court. Akbar was followed by his son Jahangir, his grandson Shah Jahan, and his great grandson, the last great Mughal emperor, Aurangzeb. By the 1700s, the Mughal dynasty was no longer powerful, and the former empire split into a land of separate kingdoms.

Emperor Akbar passes the crown to his son Jahangir in this Mughal painting.

In 1600, British merchants from the East India Company set up trading posts along India's coast. They traded silver coins and other British goods for Indian goods, including silk, a type of cotton called muslin, and spices. People in Europe needed spices, such as peppercorns, cloves, cardamom, and cinnamon, to preserve meat and hide the taste of food that had gone bad.

Capturing the subcontinent

The East India Company was more than a business. It had its own army, which gradually took over much of the subcontinent. In 1765, after defeating the troops of Mughal ruler Shah Alam II, the East India Company was given the right to collect all **revenues** from the eastern provinces of Bengal, Bihar, and Orissa.

As the East India Company continued to seize large portions of land, it collected taxes from its newly conquered territories and grew tea, which was shipped around the world, on farmland that once grew food. As a result, the people of India suffered from **famine**. The East India Company also purchased, at very cheap rates, cotton that grew in India. The cotton was sent to England to be made into cloth and then sold in India at extremely high prices. They made enormous profits and destroyed India's industries. All these actions made Indians resent the British Raj, or rule.

The Mughal ruler Shah Alam II reviews the East India Company's troops, in this engraving from 1781.

War for independence

The army of the East India Company was made up of British officers, who were in charge of local soldiers, called sepoys. On May 10, 1857, a group of sepoys in northern India received cartridges for their new rifles. They had to bite open the cartridges before loading them into the rifles, but a rumor spread that the protective grease covering the cartridges was pig or cow fat. Muslim sepoys refused to bite the cartridges because Islam does not allow its followers to eat pork. Hindu sepoys refused to bite the cartridges because, according to their beliefs, cows are sacred. Many sepoys were arrested. Two days later, Muslim and Hindu troops in Delhi rebelled against British officers to protest the arrests. The fighting spread through the north and central parts of India before the British defeated the Muslim and Hindu troops in April 1858. Many people died in what is called the First War of Independence.

The All India Muslim League

The All India Muslim League was founded by a group of Muslims in 1906. Members of the League wanted the subcontinent to be free of British rule. They also wanted to protect the rights of Muslims in an independent country. A famous poet and philosopher who belonged to the League, Dr. Muhammad Iqbal, suggested that parts of India with large Muslim populations should form an independent nation, separate from India. In 1940, Muhammad Ali Jinnah, the League's leader, presented a **resolution** at the League's annual meeting announcing the plan to divide the country. The League unanimously passed the resolution, which is called the Pakistan Resolution. It was the beginning of the founding of Pakistan.

Muhammad Ali Jinnah (1876–1948) became the first governor general of Pakistan. Today, Pakistanis refer to him as **Quaid-e-Azam***, or "Great Leader." His picture hangs in government offices and many homes. After only a year as ruler of the independent nation that he helped create, Jinnah died of tuberculosis.*

Partition and independence

People in India disagreed about whether their country should be divided. This caused the tension between Muslims and Hindus to worsen, and there were many violent conflicts. In 1946, fighting broke out between the two groups in Calcutta, India, and 5,000 people were killed. To avoid a **civil war**, the British decided to partition, or divide, India into two countries — Pakistan, which would have a Muslim majority, and India, which would be home to mostly Hindus and **Sikhs**. Both countries were granted independence from Britain.

A new country

Members of the All Indian Muslim League demonstrate in London, England in 1946. They supported the partition of India and the creation of the state of Pakistan.

On August 14, 1947, Pakistan became a country. It was made up of two areas, West Pakistan and East Pakistan, that were nearly 1,000 miles (1,600 kilometers) apart. India lay between these two areas, each of which had a large number of Muslims. Although they shared a religion, the people of East and West Pakistan had distinct **cultures** and spoke different languages.

Partition caused the largest movement of people in history as people left their new countries, fearing for their safety. About 7.5 million Muslims in India left for Pakistan, and about 10 million Hindus and Sikhs, who found themselves living in Pakistan, left for India. More than one million Hindus, Sikhs, and Muslims were killed during violent clashes as they traveled past one another in cities where the groups used to live side by side.

Getting started

The government of the new country faced many challenges. India's government had agreed to give Pakistan 20 percent of its property, including machinery, library books, and weapons. Some divisions were awkward, for example, dictionaries or cases of encyclopedias were split in half. At first, Pakistan's new leaders had only a few offices and little furniture. Some even had to work in tents for months, without desks, telephones, or electricity.

Muhammad Ali Jinnah had wanted the new country to be a democracy, where leaders were elected by the people of Pakistan. This was written into the country's first constitution in 1956. After Jinnah's death, not all of Pakistan's leaders followed the constitution. Some military generals declared **martial law**. They abolished elections and ruled with the help of the military.

Bangladesh

East Pakistan was smaller in size than West Pakistan, but more people lived there. People in East Pakistan were upset that their country's new capital was Karachi, on the south coast of West Pakistan, and they felt left out of important political decisions. In addition, they were angry that East Pakistan was becoming poorer, while West Pakistan was becoming wealthier.

In 1970, a cyclone and tidal wave struck East Pakistan, killing more than 200,000 people. Many survivors felt great resentment toward West Pakistan because they believed it had not sent East Pakistan food and other supplies quickly enough. In March 1971, East Pakistan declared itself an independent state. Indian troops helped East Pakistanis defend themselves from troops sent by West Pakistan. In December 1971, India defeated West Pakistan. East Pakistan became the country of Bangladesh, and West Pakistan became the Pakistan we know today.

Martial law

After losing Bangladesh, Pakistanis elected a new prime minister, Zulfiqar Ali Bhutto, who worked hard to improve schools and hospitals in the country. In 1977, after Bhutto was accused of arranging the results of an election, General Muhammad Zia ul-Haq used the military to seize control of the country and declared himself the new president. He accused Bhutto of ordering another politician's murder, and in 1979, Bhutto was hanged. Zia continued to run Pakistan under martial law. He did not call an election to let Pakistanis choose their own leader until 1988.

More turmoil

In August 1988, three months before the election, Zia died in a plane crash. In November, Pakistanis elected the daughter of Zulfiqar Ali Bhutto, Benazir Bhutto, as their new prime minister. She was the first female leader of a modern Muslim state. At first, Benazir Bhutto was very popular because she tried to improve people's standards of living, but she found it difficult to make changes. In 1990, she lost an election to Nawaz Sharif. She was reelected from 1993 to 1996,

when Sharif once again became prime minister. On October 12, 1999, General Pervez Musharraf and the military seized power from Nawaz Sharif and restored martial law. Pakistanis still live under martial law, although Musharraf has promised a return to democracy.

Kashmir

Before partition, the *maharajah*, or ruler, of Kashmir was asked whether he wanted the northeast tip of West Pakistan to remain part of India or join the new country of Pakistan. The population of Kashmir was 85 percent Muslim, but the *maharajah* was Hindu. He had still not decided what to do two months after Pakistan and India became independent countries.

Muslim Kashmiris worried that their *maharajah* would choose to remain with India. With the help of Muslims from a newly partitioned Pakistan, they rebelled. India sent troops into Kashmir to stop the fighting, but it continued until 1949, when the **United Nations** arranged a **cease-fire**. Kashmir ended up divided along the line where Pakistan and India stopped fighting, with one-third in Pakistan and two-thirds in India.

The United Nations suggested that the people of Kashmir vote to decide which country they wanted to join. In 1965, after India refused to allow the Kashmiris to vote, Indian and Pakistani troops fought in Kashmir again. The United Nations arranged another cease-fire. Today, troops from both countries guard their part of Kashmir against attempts by the other country to take control of their land.

As prime minister of Pakistan, Benazir Bhutto worked hard to improve health care and provide education for all children.

11

Around 140 million people live in Pakistan, while millions of Pakistanis live in other countries. Most Pakistanis are Muslims, but they belong to a number of **sects** that have somewhat different beliefs. About 77 percent of Muslims in Pakistan are Sunnis, and 20 percent are Shias.

According to Sunnis, after Muhammad died, the leaders of the Muslim world were caliphs, who were elected. Shias believed that only Muhammad's **descendants** could be the true leaders of Islam. According to a large sect of Shias, called the "Twelvers," the last, or twelfth, leader disappeared in the 800s. They believe that Allah has kept him alive, and that someday he will reappear and bring peace to the world. There are other differences between Sunnis and Shias, including the fact that they do not have the same *hadiths*. *Hadiths* are collections of Muhammad's sayings and traditions, which guide Muslim law.

These boys, who live on Pakistan's border with Afghanistan, are heading to the market to buy eggplants to pickle in oil.

*Punjabis are famous for creating beautiful crafts such as carved wooden furniture and colorful cloth, used to make this Punjabi woman's **dupatta**, or scarf.*

Punjabis

Punjabis, Sindhis, Pathans, and Baluchis are among Pakistan's major groups. All these groups are Sunni Muslims. Punjabis live mostly in the province of Punjab and speak different **dialects** of the Punjabi language. They are the largest group of people in Pakistan, forming more than half the population. Traditionally, each Punjabi belonged to a tribe or clan, called a *qaum*. These tribes still exist in some rural areas. People in one *qaum* have the same ancestors and often hold similar jobs. Many Punjabis are farmers or craftspeople, but others live in Punjab's large, modern cities and work for the government, in businesses, or in the military.

A nomadic Sindhi family rests by a covered caravan.

Sindhis

"Sindhi" is the name given to a group of people living in the province of Sind and to the language that they speak. A large group of Hindus lived in Sind before partition, and many of their customs have influenced Sindhi culture, such as putting one's palms together in greeting. Other Sindhi customs survive mainly in rural areas. They include celebrating festivals such as *Malakhara*, when men wrestle one another to the ground by holding cloths tied around their opponents' waists.

Pathans

Pathans speak Pushtu, or Pashto. They mainly work as herders and farmers in the North-West Frontier Province and northern Baluchistan, as well as in Afghanistan, where they are called Pashtuns. Some Pathans live in villages and cities in other parts of Pakistan, where they are traders, merchants, and shopkeepers, or where they work for the military or government. The tribes that live in northern Baluchistan and in Pakistan's northern mountains have their own system of government. Decisions are made by the *kashar*, or elders, and by the *jirga*, a council made up of tribal leaders. Pakistani law is not strictly enforced in these areas, and many Pathans who live there would like independence from Pakistan.

Pukhtunwali

Pathans follow a strict code of honor called *pukhtunwali*. They believe that warm hospitality should be shown to all visitors. This hospitality sometimes includes offering *melmastia*, or **sanctuary**, to people who ask for protection. Pathans who follow *pukhtunwali* also seek revenge when they, their families, or their tribe is insulted. The code of honor is so important that people born in Pathan villages who do not follow *pukhtunwali* are not considered Pathan.

Pathans claim to be descendants of Imraul Qais, who converted the Pathans to Islam after he met the prophet Muhammad. Each Pathan tribe takes its name from one of Qais' descendants.

Baluchis

The Baluchis form the second largest group of people in Baluchistan, after the Pathans. They speak various dialects of Baluchi, a language related to Persian. Some Baluchis still live traditional lifestyles as pastoral nomads. They travel with their livestock in the spring and summer to find water and food. Using twigs, branches, grass, reeds, or straw, they set up tents called *khizdi* or build huts called *jhuggi*. In the winter, they move to mud huts on the plains.

Like the Pathans, nomadic Baluchis follow the decisions of a *jirga*. Sometimes, groups of Baluchis fight for the right to govern themselves completely, without interference from Pakistan's government. In 2000, a group of Baluchis bombed an army base in Quetta, Baluchistan's capital, to protest the Pakistani government's attempt to impose laws, taxes, and elections on tribal communities.

Baltis

On the northeast tip of Pakistan, the dry, mountainous area of Baltistan is home to the Baltis. The Mughals named Baltistan "Little Tibet" because it lies near Tibet, a region in China. The Baltis, who are Shia Muslims, speak an early form of the Tibetan language and feel close ties to the people of Tibet.

Some Baltis earn a living as guides and porters for people who climb the mountains of Baltistan.

Most Baltis lead a traditional farming lifestyle, but they worry that their culture is disappearing as new roads and tourists, who climb the surrounding mountains, disturb their villages. They are trying to hold onto their traditions. For example, Balti doctors called *hakims* still cure illnesses with plants, using skills that have been passed down for generations.

Mohajirs

Urdu-speaking Muslims who traveled to Pakistan from India immediately after partition were given the name Mohajirs. *Mohajir* is the Urdu word for "refugee," or a person who leaves his or her country during a war or another dangerous time to seek safety in a new country. Many Mohajirs left India because they were worried that they and their businesses would be destroyed in the violence following partition. They settled in large cities across Sind, such as Karachi and Hyderabad, where they opened new businesses. Some Sindhis felt that the Mohajirs were taking work away from them. The tension between the two groups has sometimes led to violence.

Kalasha

Many smaller groups, such as the Kalasha and Wakhi, live throughout Pakistan. The Kalasha make their home in three small, wooded valleys between the northern mountains. They take their name from the word *kala*, meaning "black," which is the color of the long robes that Kalasha women wear. Unlike most people in Pakistan, the Kalasha are not Muslim. They practice animism, which means that they worship spirits in nature. They also believe in many gods, including Khodai who created the world.

The Kalasha sometimes face **discrimination** because they are not Muslim, so many Kalasha are **converting** to Islam, moving away from their valleys, and leaving behind their traditional lifestyle. Only 3,000 Kalasha still live in the valleys, where they grow wheat, walnuts, vegetables such as corn and **lentils**, and fruits such as peaches and apricots. They also raise sheep and goats, but not chickens. One legend warns that the Kalasha will be destroyed if they eat chicken or eggs.

Kalasha women wear a train that hangs down from their head to well below their shoulders. The train is covered with rows of cowrie shells, colored beads, and coin-shaped metal pieces. Shells were once used as currency and are seen as signs of wealth.

The Wakhi people

Hundreds of years ago, ancestors of the Wakhi moved, with their herds of animals, from the Wakhan Corridor in Afghanistan to Gojal, a grasslands area west of Baltistan. They spoke a Persian language, also called Wakhi. Today, the Wakhi continue to raise animals, such as yaks and sheep. Crops, such as wheat and apricots, are another source of food. The Wakhi are Ismailis, a group of Shias. Unlike other Shias, Ismailis believe that Muhammad's descendants are still alive. Their leader is called the Aga Khan.

Afghan refugees

Refugees from Afghanistan, the country west of Pakistan, have streamed into Pakistan for decades. Millions of Afghan refugees came to Pakistan after the Soviet Union invaded their country in 1979. Even more refugees crossed the border through mountain passes after the United States began a war against terrorists in Afghanistan in 2001. They settled in refugee camps near the passes, living in tents and shelters made from clay, mud bricks, wood, metal, and fabric. While many Afghans have returned to their homeland, others have moved to Pakistani cities. Still others remain in refugee camps.

Pakistani men wear off-white, gray, brown, or blue **shalwar-qamiz,** *while women wear* **shalwar-qamiz** *with bright colors and patterns. Women also wear wide rectangular scarves called* **dupattas,** *made of light fabrics such as cotton or chiffon.*

If you travel across Pakistan, you will notice that people in each region wear different styles of clothes. Pathan women in the north and northwest wear long dresses of all colors over a loose pair of trousers called a *shalwar*. Women in Sind wear shirts embroidered with beautifully colored patterns over their *shalwar*. In warmer parts of the country, such as the hot, dry plains of Baluchistan, people keep cool by wearing loose-fitting clothing, which is often white to reflect the sunlight. Both men and women in large cities wear western-style clothing, as well as Pakistani fashions.

In fashion

Many men and women throughout Pakistan dress in a *shalwar-qamiz*, which consists of a long shirt called a *qamiz* worn over a *shalwar*. A *kurta* is a looser version of the *qamiz*. Many *shalwar-qamiz* are made to measure by tailors working in **bazaars**. Some *shalwar-qamiz* are made of light, thin cotton that is cool in hot weather. Others are made of heavier cotton, wool, or silk.

Caps and turbans

To figure out what part of Pakistan a man comes from, look at his head. Men from Sind wear round cloth caps, called *topi*, that take skilled craftspeople up to a month to sew. In northern Pakistan, men wear a variety of woolen caps with rolled brims. Other Pakistani men wear turbans, which are long pieces of cloth wound around the head or wrapped around a skull cap called a *kulla*. Many Pakistani men in cities do not wear caps or turbans at all.

Topi *caps are embroidered with thread and have tiny mirrors, beads, or small shells stitched into them.*

Many Muslims believe that white is the holiest color for turbans because, according to legend, the prophet Muhammad wore a white turban.

Scarfs and shawls

Many women wear a long, wide scarf called a *dupatta* over their shoulders or on their heads when they go outside because Islam requires them to protect their **modesty**. Wealthy women wear shawls from Kashmir that are called *shatoosh*, ring, or *pashmina* shawls. These shawls are made from *pashmina*, which is the fleece, or wool, of the Tibetan antelope. The fleece is finer than human hair, and the shawls are so thin that they can pass through finger rings.

Purdah

Some Muslim Pakistani women dress according to a practice called *purdah*, which means "veil" or "curtain." To live in *purdah* means that women must not be seen by men who are not their relatives. When male visitors come to their homes, they stay in another room. If they leave

their homes, they cover their heads and bodies with a long, loose garment called a *burqah* to protect their modesty. A *burqah* might be white, black, purple, or bright blue. One part of the *burqah* is a long-sleeved cloak that covers the body; the other part is a headpiece. Some headpieces have three veils, each of which covers a different part of the face. Women often remove the veil over the eyes to see better. In some areas, especially large cities, many women do not wear *burqahs* because they consider them old-fashioned. Women who farm also do not wear *burqahs* because it would make it more difficult for them to do their work.

Some **burqahs** *have headpieces that fit tightly over the head. The woman looks through a net that covers her face.*

17

Village life

In Pakistani villages, children do not only live with their mothers, fathers, brothers, and sisters, but also with their aunts, uncles, cousins, and grandparents. Family members share two- or three-room houses made of bricks, clay, or sun-dried mud. Some regions have unique styles of homes. The Kalasha, who live in narrow valleys, build some of their homes up steep hillsides, one on top of another. The roof of one house is the veranda of the house above it. The villagers of Gondrani, in Baluchistan, have adapted to their surroundings in another way. Their village lies in a narrow gorge between two rocky cliffs. The villagers live in cave houses built into the cliffs, with walkways connecting the homes.

At work

Some people in villages work as tailors, barbers, mechanics, blacksmiths, or craftspeople. Others run teashops, where fresh tea is brewed in large, metal **samovars**. Many villagers farm and herd animals. On small farms, most work is done by hand, not by machine. Animals, such as oxen, help farmers plow their fields and pull wooden carts filled with crops to the village market. Women help men work in the fields, but they also prepare the day's meals, which includes grinding wheat into flour and churning milk into butter. In village homes without running water, women walk to rivers or public taps to collect water for drinking, cooking, and bathing.

(top) Homes in the Upper Swat Valley are often built with flat roofs. Fruits such as apricots can be spread on the roofs to dry in the sun.

Children's chores

Village children do many important chores. Some sweep the yard and splash water on the ground to settle dust and cool the air. Others watch over herds of sheep or yaks and help their parents care for crops. In the village of Askole, in Baltistan, children help with the wheat harvest. Before the wheat is **threshed**, they lay the cut and dried stalks down the sides of small hills and slide down.

At play

At the end of a busy day, villagers gather to play cards, talk and drink tea in teashops, or listen to *qawwali* singers, who sing religious songs. Children fly kites and play games, such as tag. After dinner, watching television is a favorite activity. Many channels show religious programs with sermons or readings from the *Qur'an*, along with films in English and Urdu, children's programs, comedy shows, and game shows.

A young boy watches as his mother and sisters wash clothes in the village of Ibrahim Hyderi, in Sind. Some families earn extra money by washing clothes for other people.

Teashops are places to get together with friends and share news. This temporary teashop has been set up at a market in northern Sind, where farmers gather to talk and to bargain for the best prices for cattle, goats, and sheep.

City life

(above) Over 14 million people live in Karachi, Pakistan's largest city.

People crowd the streets of Pakistan's large cities. Some rush off to work in government buildings, banks, hospitals, schools, and airports. Others run their own businesses, from small newsstands to large factories. After work, people sometimes go to restaurants that serve traditional Pakistani food, hamburgers, or pizza. Many people visit the tombs of **Sufi** saints, where they pray, talk with friends, and relax. Others wait in front of theaters to see movies in English, Urdu, Punjabi, or Sindhi, or they flock to see rock bands, such as Junoon, perform.

Bazaars

The smells of spices and barbecuing meat float over customers wandering through Pakistan's many bazaars. Vendors along the narrow streets call out to customers, advertising their wares. Pots, pans, gold jewelry, musical instruments, carpets, and leather shoes and bags crowd tables and the ground. Vendors selling similar items sit in a long row. If one vendor does not have what a customer wants, he yells for a nearby vendor to bring it.

Most vendors are helpful and friendly, and invite customers to drink tea with them. As they sip their tea, they bargain over the price of goods, especially expensive items such as handmade carpets. The bargaining sometimes lasts for hours, with the customer and vendor debating the price, talking about other subjects, and then returning to the debate. In addition to bazaars, people in cities go to small shops or malls where everything from shoes to televisions are sold.

(below) City dwellers buy fresh fruit and vegetables from this farmers' market in Islamabad.

An artificial lake in the Shalimar Gardens, east of Lahore, is a great place to cool off.

Keeping cool

During Pakistan's hot summer evenings, many people use electric ceiling fans to keep cool, or they sit on their flat roofs or verandas and chat with friends. Sometimes, they even sleep there on *charpoys*, which are beds made from woven ropes tied around a wooden frame.

Badgirs, or wind collectors, rise from rooftops in cities such as Thatta and Hyderabad, in Sind. Even though both these cities are close to the blisteringly hot Thar Desert, for 40 days a year, cool winds from the northeast blow over them. The *badgirs*, which look like chimneys, are really ventilation shafts that funnel the cooling breezes into houses.

Paintings of Pakistani movie stars and scenes from well-known movies decorate the outside of a cinema in Karachi.

City homes

Unlike children in Pakistani villages, children in cities often live only with their parents, brothers, and sisters. Most people live in one- or two-story homes, sometimes with small grassy plots in the front or back where flowers or bushes grow. Wealthy families live in larger homes with expensive Asian carpets, air conditioning, gardens, and swimming pools. Some homes in old parts of cities are *havelis*, traditional Mughal homes with two or three floors. *Havelis*, which get their name from the Persian word for "enclosed space," are built around central courtyards with gardens or fountains. Families with little money live on the outskirts of cities in two- or three-room houses made of mud, concrete, wood, cardboard, or plastic.

Some neighborhoods in cities, called *muhallas*, are surrounded by high fences. At one time, everyone in a *muhalla* was related, so women in *purdah* were able to walk around without wearing *burqahs*. Today, many *muhallas* are more like neighborhoods, where not all families are related, but women there still practice *purdah* less strictly than women outside *muhallas*.

Going to school

Schools in Pakistani cities look much like those in North America, while schools in villages can be as tiny as one room or as large as a few small buildings. Some villages do not have a school, so students learn outside, sitting on the ground around a teacher. During the cool winter months, they take a holiday, then return to classes in the spring.

Some children in Pakistan do not go to school at all. Children in the countryside might help their families with farmwork, while children in the city may weave carpets or work at other jobs to help their families earn extra money.

(below) Some children go to the local mosque after their regular school day to learn how to read the **Qur'an,** *which is written in Arabic.*

(above) Many schoolchildren, such as these girls in Sherqillah, in the Northern Areas, wear uniforms, such as orange or blue **shalwar-qamiz.**

Recess

During recess, some Pakistani children read and exchange comic books and story books. Others run around the schoolyard, playing games such as soccer, cricket, and tag. In one challenging game of tag called *langra sheer*, or "limping lion," the player who is "it" stands on one leg and hops around trying to tag out the other players.

A nervous time

When students complete secondary school, which they attend from the ages of thirteen to fifteen, they must pass an examination, called the Secondary School Certificate (S.S.C.), before continuing their education. They write the exam in April or May and wait all summer to find out the results. Students who pass the S.S.C. may go to a technical secondary school, where they learn a **trade**, or to a higher secondary school in preparation for college or university.

Boys study chemistry at a private college in Islamabad.

Many types of schools

Most Pakistani children attend government-run public schools in which most subjects are taught in Urdu. In towns and cities, wealthier children attend expensive private schools where they are taught in English. There are also special schools, called *madrasas*, that teach children more about Islam than other schools do. Most *madrasas* are in the countryside.

School day

Boys and girls attend school together for the first few years. Then, they are divided into separate classes. They arrive at school around 8:30 a.m. and stay until 1:00 or 2:00 p.m. When their teacher enters the classroom, the children stand up and say, "*Salaam alaikum,*" or "Peace be with you," as a sign of respect. They take courses in math, history, science, geography, Islam, physical education, Urdu, English, and sometimes the language of their region.

Students chat outside Punjab University in Lahore, the oldest university in Pakistan.

Fun and games

On Sundays, Pakistanis take a break from work and school. They go to parks where they have picnics, swim, and fly kites, which they buy or make out of colorful tissue paper, glue, and sticks. Both children and adults also enjoy playing and watching cricket, field hockey, soccer, and polo.

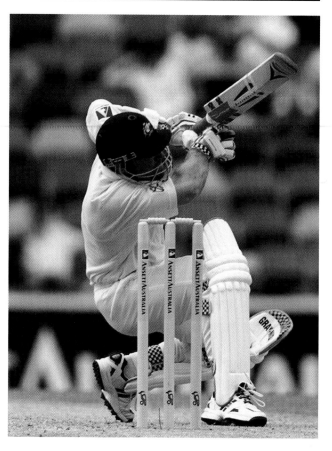

A professional cricket player, dressed in the traditional white uniform, ducks to avoid the ball during a test, or match.

Up to five children can ride the decorated camels at Clifton Beach, in Karachi.

Cricket

Cricket is a British game that is similar to baseball. A "bowler" from one team and a batter, or "striker," from another team each stand at a wicket. A wicket is made from three upright sticks with two sticks on top. Another member of the striker's team, a nonstriker, stands at the wicket near the bowler. The bowler tries to knock down the wicket by the striker with a small, heavy ball. If he or she is successful, the striker is out. If the striker hits the ball far, the striker and nonstriker run between the wickets as many times as possible before a fielder returns the ball. The team that scores the most runs at the end of the match wins.

An ancient sport

People in Pakistan still play a game, polo, that was popular in Central Asia over 2,000 years ago. Pakistani polo games require two teams of six players each. The players race their horses down a long field, using mallets to try to hit a ball between the other team's goal posts.

In the central and southern parts of Pakistan, polo is played by the wealthy. In the north, polo is popular with anyone who can afford a horse. Polo matches in the north are especially exciting to watch. They are fast and rough, with the horses colliding as players swing them around quickly to get the ball. Large crowds press close to the low wall that surrounds the polo field, and drummers and flutists play songs that get faster and louder when a goal is scored or is about to be scored.

A polo team in Gilgit practices for a match against players from Chitral. The match is part of a three-day polo festival in the Shandur Pass, in the north.

Kabaddi

Kabaddi players need to be in good shape. Not only do they run, wrestle, and dodge other players, but they must be able to hold their breath. During a game of *kabaddi*, a player from one team runs into the other team's territory, where he tries to touch one or more players. Once he tags them, he must run quickly back into his territory, all in the space of one breath! If he does, the players he tagged are out. If the players from the other team hold him in their territory until he runs out of breath, he is out. The player proves that he is not taking a breath by saying the word *kabaddi* over and over again.

Kabaddi *is popular outside Pakistan, in countries such as Nepal, Bangladesh, and India. In southern India, the sport is known as* **Chedugudu** *or* **Hu-Tu-Tu,** *and in eastern India it is known as* **Hadudu** *or* **Chu-Kit-Kit.**

Hot and spicy

Pakistan's early Muslim rulers, the Mughals, loved elaborately prepared dishes. They feasted on spicy, rich food that people in Pakistan, especially in Punjab, still eat today. "Mughal food" is flavored with chili, cinnamon, cloves, cardamom, black pepper, cumin, coriander, and golden-colored saffron, which is made from the **stigmas** of crocuses. Spices are sometimes added to *achars*, which are fruits and vegetables, such as eggplants, limes, and lemons, that are pickled in oil. To cool their mouths from the spicy flavors, Pakistanis often eat crunchy, refreshing green peppers and plenty of yogurt.

On the menu

Breakfasts in Pakistan are often small, consisting of a cup of tea, an egg, and *roti*, or bread. For lunch and dinner, people enjoy dishes such as *korma*, which is spiced meat in a thick gravy mixed with yogurt; *kofta*, which are like meatballs; and vegetables such as spinach, okra, potatoes, green beans, and eggplant that are eaten on their own or with meat. People in cities stop at food stands to buy *samosas*, which are minced meat or vegetables wrapped in a thin, crispy pastry. They also buy *kebabs*. *Kebabs* are made of minced meat and are either cooked on skewers over coals or fried like meat patties.

Tandoori style

One way that Pakistanis prepare chicken is in a *tandoor*. A *tandoor* is a red-hot clay, metal, or stone oven that is built into the ground. *Tandoori* chicken, which is soaked in yogurt and rubbed with spices, is very tender because the temperature in a *tandoor* is several degrees hotter than in a normal oven. The chicken cooks more quickly and does not dry out.

Curries

Many people think that curry is a spice, but in fact, the word refers to a *masala,* or mixture of spices, that includes cumin, coriander, and turmeric. These spices are mixed with onions, tomatoes, and meat to create different dishes, which are also called curries. For example, *dhal* is lentil curry and *machli ka salan* is fish curry. On special occasions, Pakistanis eat curries served with raisins, cashews, pistachios, eggs, and lettuce; but they also eat curries every day at home and as fast food.

(left) Women from the Hunza Valley sort dried apricots. During cold winters in the valley, the dried apricots are mixed with snow to make a type of ice cream.

*(opposite) Vendors called spice **wallahs** sell blends of spices called **masalas**. Some **masalas** are standard mixtures of spices, but others are family recipes that are passed down from generation to generation.*

Bread basket

Rotis of all kinds are an important part of most meals. *Chapatis* are a type of flatbread, while *parathas* are thicker and flakier because oil is added to the dough during cooking. *Parathas* are sometimes stuffed with minced meat and vegetables. *Naan* is the largest type of *roti*. It is like a soft, thick pancake that was once most commonly eaten by Pathans. Today, it is popular everywhere. To make *naan*, a breadmaker called a *tandoori* kneads flour with milk, yogurt, and eggs. The *tandoori* then throws the dough against the hot sides of a *tandoor* with iron tongs.

Rice

Rice is good for soaking up the sauces that cover Pakistani foods. Almost every day, Pakistanis eat plain white rice or sweet rice seasoned with cloves, cardamom, or cinnamon. They also mix rice with meat, vegetables, raisins, and nuts to make a dish called *pilau*. *Biryani*, which is rice cooked in meat sauce, is often served on special occasions. The plates of *biryani* are sometimes decorated with pieces of edible silver paper tinted yellow with saffron.

Balls of dough are rolled into thin teardrop shapes before they are cooked to make **naan**. *The perfect* **naan** *has a bubbled top and toasted marks on the bottom from the heat of the* **tandoor** *oven.*

Washing it down

Pakistanis drink many kinds of tea, including jasmine tea; Kashmiri tea, which has raisins and nuts; and green tea with sugar and cracked cardamom seeds. A common black tea, called *masala chai*, is brewed with milk and sweetened heavily with spices such as nutmeg, cinnamon, or cloves. Fruit drinks, called squashes, and *lassi*, which is yogurt or buttermilk mixed with water, are also popular. People believe that the yogurt drink soothes their stomach. Pakistanis also drink lemonade and soda, like people in other parts of the world.

Satisfying a sweet tooth

After the main course, Pakistanis often eat desserts of fresh or dried fruit. Sweeter treats include *ras gulla*, which are cheese balls covered in a sugary syrup, and *jalebi*, which are deep-fried spirals made of flour, also dipped in a sugary syrup. Pakistanis also eat rice puddings, such as *kheer* and *firni*, and tapiocas that smell like perfume because rose water has been added to them. Children like to snack on chocolate and all types of candies.

A mother serves a curry dish made from meat, chickpeas, and a mixture of spices to her family for dinner.

Carrot *halva*

Halva is a sweet, thick pudding made from grated vegetables, fruits, or grains, such as semolina. You can make carrot *halva* with an adult's help.

You will need:
- 6 medium carrots, grated
- 3 cups (.75 L) whole milk
- 3 teaspoons (15 ml) cardamom
- large saucepan
- 1/4 cup (50 ml) vegetable oil
- 1 tablespoon (15 ml) raisins
- 1 tablespoon (15 ml) coarsely chopped pistachios (optional)

*Paan is a Pakistani treat sold by street vendors called **paan wallahs**. A leaf from a betel plant is wrapped in a triangle around crushed rose petals, coconut flakes, and spices such as cardamom and cloves. A sweet-flavored **paan** is called **meetha**, and a spicier version with tobacco paste is called **sada**.*

What to do:
1. Combine carrots, milk, and cardamom in a large, heavy saucepan. Bring to a boil over medium heat.

2. Cook for at least 30 minutes, stirring occasionally, until there is no liquid left. You might need to lower the heat to prevent the carrots from burning.

3. Add the oil to the carrot mixture. Cook for about 10 to 15 minutes until it turns a rich, reddish orange color and is no longer watery.

4. Add sugar, raisins, and pistachios, if you are using them. Cook for 5 minutes longer.

5. Serve the *halva* warm, or pour it into a serving dish, refrigerate, and then cut the *halva* into bars.

Pakistanis often give sweets to friends and neighbors on special occasions, such as marriages, births, or children passing exams.

 # A great team

Huma wakes up when the yak-hair rug that she sleeps on tickles her cheek. She sees her mother preparing breakfast by the cast iron stove. Huma's heart races when she remembers what day it is. July 11! *Salgirah*! On *Salgirah*, the whole village of Shimshal and every other Ismaili community in Pakistan celebrate the day when their religious leader, Prince Karim Aga Khan, became the Aga Khan, after his grandfather.

Huma's mother sees that she is awake and says, "Huma, please go and get some wood for the stove, and find your brother." "Yes, *Nan*," Huma replies, grabbing the bright blue *shalwar-qamiz* that she wears to school.

Huma spots her brother, Ashraf, moving toward the mud by the tiny **irrigation** stream that waters their small wheat and bean fields. "You can't play in the mud in your school uniform!" she warns. His *shalwar-qamiz* is a blue-gray color.

(top) **Huma and her classmates, dressed in their school uniforms, walk to the Salgirah celebration.**

Ashraf follows Huma up a wooden ladder and onto the flat roof of their stone house, where they keep the firewood. As Huma collects the wood, Ashraf runs over to the smokehole in the roof and dangles his foot over the edge. "*Nan*!" he calls down the smokehole. "Look at me!" Huma sighs and says, "Come *on*, Ashraf."

She will not let him ruin her day. This afternoon, she and four other girls from her school are performing a drama, or skit, in front of the whole village with some boys from the boys' school, including Ashraf. Huma wants to impress her father, who is highly respected in the village. Last winter, he and five other men took the yaks from the village to pastures high in the surrounding mountains, where they kept them safe for the winter.

Huma and Ashraf eat *chapatis* for breakfast with their mother, father, aunt, and two cousins, who live with them. "I'll be watching for your drama!" their father says to them as they head off to school.

Huma's father herds a yak to higher pastures in the mountains. Yaks are important to Shimshalis, who milk them, make cheese from their milk, and weave rugs from their hair.

After the children arrive at the girls' and boys' schools, teachers lead them to the courtyard of the community hall, where most people from the village are gathered. A picture of the Aga Khan sits on a wooden throne, and villagers give speeches about what has happened in the village during the past year. Prayers are recited between the speeches. Huma fidgets because she can't wait to perform her drama.

After a lunch of *bhat*, a cooked paste made from flour, water, and yak butter, the celebration moves to a nearby field. The men of the village dance. Then, schoolchildren sing songs and perform dramas. Many dramas are about the village and make the audience laugh.

Finally, it is Huma's turn. She and the other girls pretend to be the women from their village who herd the goats and sheep in the lower pastures during the summer. Ashraf and some boys from his school are the goats and sheep. Most of the boys cooperate, but Ashraf bounds away from Huma, just like a real goat. Huma is angry and runs after her brother. Then, she hears the audience laughing. Her father's laughter is louder than anyone else's. He likes the drama! When Huma chases Ashraf back into the group of boys, everyone claps.

Afterward, Huma and Ashraf watch boys from the village's gymnastics club dive through a hoop of fire. They also watch their father's team win a tug-of-rope contest. Before the contest starts, many women tie their *dupattas* around their husbands' waists for luck, including Huma's *nan*. At the end of the day, the whole family returns home, tired and happy. They eat sweets sent by Huma's uncle, who works in a bank in a nearby city. Huma's father looks at Huma and Ashraf and says, "You two make a great team."

Huma smiles at her brother and admits, "I think we do, too."

Men from Shimshal, including Huma's father, show their strength in a tug-of-war contest.

Glossary

bazaar An area of small shops and stalls

cease-fire An agreement between two countries to stop fighting and discuss peace

civil war A war between different groups of people within a country

convert To change one's religion, faith, or beliefs

culture The customs, beliefs, and arts of a distinct group of people

descendent A person who can trace his or her family roots to a certain family or group

dialect A version of a language spoken in one region

discrimination The act of treating people unfairly because of race, religion, gender, or other factors

famine An extreme shortage of food in a country or large area

fertile Able to produce abundant crops or vegetation

homeland A country that is identified with a particular people or ethnic group

irrigation The process of supplying water to land using ditches, sprinklers, and other means

lentil A round seed that can be eaten

martial law Political rule by military authorities, especially in times of war or crisis

modesty The state of dressing and acting in a proper, respectable way

monastery A building where monks live and work according to religious rules

mosque A sacred building in which Muslims worship

Muslim A person who follows the religion of Islam

plague A fatal disease that spreads quickly

plain A large area of flat land

plateau An area of flat land that is higher than the surrounding land

prophet A person who is believed to speak on behalf of God

resolution A formal statement or opinion decided by an assembly or parliament

revenue A government's income that is collected through taxes and fees

samovar A metal urn with a tap, used for boiling water for tea

sanctuary A safe place for someone in danger

sect A religious group that is divided from a larger group

Sikh A follower of the Indian religion Sikhism, which developed from Hinduism

stigma The central part of a flower, which contains pollen

subcontinent A large landmass that is part of a continent, but is considered independent

Sufi A member of a Muslim religious group who tries to concentrate on pure thoughts by living a simple life and praying

thresh To separate grain from straw

trade A job that involves special skill or training

United Nations An international organization that promotes peace

 # Index

1 2 3 4 5 6 7 8 9 0   Printed in the USA   0 9 8 7 6 5 4 3 2